Smelly Stories

of
Giants, Goblins and Nincompoops

To Ivy

EVELYN WINTERS

Evelyn Winters

Love

The Evelyn Winters Adventure

Hold your noses…

Stories in this book

The Little Big Clockmaker   17

A Very Giant Tale   41

The Blessington Dolls   69

An Imp Called Boo   107

Hodgepodge   129

This way for a tour of the ancient city of Chester!

We start with Chester's most iconic landmark.

The Little Big Clockmaker

Dedicated to Caiden

Edited by
Robin Chambers

Egan Bagley is a talented clockmaker who is about to create one of the most magnificent clocks the country has ever set its eyes on, but after a visit from a gypsy selling him a bewitched bead…

…things are about to turn peculiar!

With the magical powers of the four faced clock, the little gnome of a man plays havoc with time and is about to become one of the richest men in Chester with upsetting consequences.

This way...

The Little
BIG CLOCKMAKER

Once upon a time, many years ago when clocks ticked much louder, there lived a talented clockmaker in an enchanted walled city in the northwest of England. The elf-like man was a master craftsman with an exceptional gift. He had served many a crowned head, but his latest assignment was to be his greatest. Egan Bagley was to create one of the most magnificent clocks the country had ever set eyes on.

The third Duke of Meadowsville had ordered the clocksmith to create something spectacular: to make the city look more beautiful. For a hundred days and a hundred nights, Egan shut himself away in his dusty workshop, leaving no window uncovered and no door unlocked as he carried out his top-secret work.

One hot night, while tapping, hammering, carving and crafting one of the four intricate faces of the massive clock, he became exhausted. The heat made him feel weak, but he couldn't stop. He feared he would not meet his deadline, and failed to notice a shrunken woman with twisted fingers suddenly standing behind him and clutching a tattered bag. She exhaled – a drawn out rasping sound – which stopped him in his tracks. He

spun, nearly losing his balance on his old rickety ladder, and his brass tweezers tinkled to the ground.

"You shouldn't be in here!" he complained.

The peculiar visitor simply observed him and held out her shabby bag. Flummoxed by her presence, Egan raised his eyebrows, peering over his large round glasses. He was sure he had locked his door.

"What do you want?" he snapped.

"Buy a bead from a gypsy, sir?" she finally asked. Her gravelly voice grated in the workshop's dry air.

Egan sighed in relief and hurried down his ladder. "Yes, yes, if I must," he grabbed a coin and tossed it to the old woman who caught it as if by instinct. She rooted in her bag and brought out a speckled red bead.

"Keep this safe and your gift as a clockmaker will become… extraordinary." She placed it on his palm and closed his hand around it. He would never forget that moment. Her hands were unnaturally cold in the sweltering heat of the night.

Having no idea what she could have meant, he took the bead over to his bench and placed it securely in his tin of tools. He turned to thank her but she'd gone as fast as she'd come. He rushed to the door which was closed and locked. Thinking he'd been hallucinating, he dashed back over to the tin. The bead twinkled wondrously in the light of the worktop lantern.

Days later, he finished the clock's mechanism and carefully pieced the parts together. He wound the handle of the giant clock and proudly listened to its noisy tick. It looked wonderful. He had never made anything so spectacular. All he had to do was paint it…

But time was ticking. He ran up the ladders and removed all four clock-face hands for painting. The deadline was today and he felt anxious the Duke would send someone to find him.

All that day he did not stop, and into the night, and the following day and all the following night… Finally the work of genius towered before him in its full splendour. With all its hands securely back on its faces and with its glorious red and gold detail, incredible ironwork and prominent green copper ogee copula, it surpassed anything the little gnome of a man had ever done or seen before.

And not a moment too soon… There was a thunderous knock on his door: the knock he'd been dreading. He had missed the deadline and feared the wrath of the Duke.

He unlocked and pulled open the heavy door to see the great man standing there with two of his guards. The silken-suited lord rushed past, eager to see his timepiece. He stopped and stared for some time, while Egan waited with baited breath…

"EGAN BAGLEY!" he finally bellowed. Egan flinched. "Y-Y-Yes," he stammered.

"It's…" the third duke wavered, drawing his eyes away from the clock and resting them on Egan. "It's **PERFECT**! This **IS** the Eastgate Clock! Just what the city needs. It will catch the eye of the tourists! It will cause unrest amongst the residents."

He grabbed the clockmaker's hand and shook it furiously. "It is garish, almost shocking; but **OUTSTANDING** man. Well done!"

Egan wasn't sure if that was good or bad; but the Duke seemed happy. "I'm sorry for missing the deadline," he said in a rush, "but you see, I had to ensure the quality and detail were just right….."

"What are you talking about?" the Duke cut in. "You are on time. To be perfectly honest I didn't expect you to have such a magnificent piece of work completed on schedule."

"What day is it?" Egan asked.

"Friday; it's Friday, my dear fellow," laughed the Duke.

"Forgive me sir, I thought it was Sunday. I must have lost track of time…"

That night, alone and confused, the clockmaker stared at the four faces above him. He was sure of the days. He'd bought a paper that morning and the date was there clear as day, held tightly in his blistered hand: **SUNDAY**…

Like a man possessed, he threw the paper down, sprang from the crate he sat on and ran up each of the wooden ladders in turn. One by one he removed the blackened hands and placed them in his tool box next to the shrunken woman's speckled red bead. Then he went home to sleep.

Any reasonable person might be forgiven for thinking he was losing his mind, but Egan Bagley considered it a stroke of genius. Surely no-one else could have come to such a conclusion…

There was a chance, just the merest possibility, that his talents as a clockmaker were now **SO** exceptional that he had – probably, possibly or perhaps even maybe:

STOPPED TIME!

Everything appeared normal. Life went on, but when he returned the clock hands to the four faces it became Friday again. He opened his tin of tools and the bewitched bead winked at him. He thought about discarding it but temptation stopped him. There were a few things he could try before throwing it away. With the clock hands safely packed away in the tin, he set off home.

The next day he passed the city's racecourse and watched thoughtfully from the city walls. It was race day, and he had an idea. He would get the names of all the winners, return to the workshop the next day and replace all the clock hands so the day would revert to Friday. Then he would place several bets at the local bookmakers.

As before, the day returned to Friday. He did not see it happen, he did not feel it happen, and he did not know how it could have happened…

But it just did.

He placed a small bet on each of the winning horses, rushed back to the workshop and took off the hands of the clock once more, placing them away in their usual place. The following afternoon he checked the results and returned to the bookmakers to pick up his winnings.

It had worked! He could hardly believe it.

Egan went back to the bookmakers. This time he placed all his winnings on the same winning horses. He was about to make himself one of the richest men in the city. "Just one more bet…" he told himself, and then he would throw the winking bead away.

This time he collected an absolute fortune and attracted a good deal of attention; but as soon as he repositioned the hands on the clock everybody promptly forgot about it. Back in the workshop he remembered his dreams – the ones he'd had when he worked the livelong days – of silken suits and a splendid house, and travelling the world in exclusive luxury, the envy of one and all.

That was what he was going to do, starting tomorrow. Greed had got the better of him, you see, and he placed more bets and went on placing bets until he had… **MILLIONS!**

He purchased a much sought-after home by the river and spent money like water. He frittered away thousands on the finest clothes. He had servants, overflowing fountains and everything he could ever want. His wealth became renowned.

No-one could fathom how a humble clockmaker could be so well-off…

Of course it didn't stop there. For his own amusement, he entered and won many local competitions. There was no real competition in the longest beard contest, especially when he meddled with time like he did, but he also swept the board in the general knowledge quizzes in all the local pubs. His knowledge on a whole host of topics appeared comprehensive and accurate. He soon acquired the nickname 'Professor Rich'.

People would stop him in the street and ask: "How do you know everything?" and then "Can you spare some change?" Strangely, he never gave them anything. Not one penny…

Spoiled by all that fortune and fame, Egan forgot all about his original plan to dispose of the bead and return to his old life. He went on a Grand Tour of the whole world, living like a king the entire time…

But a day came when he replaced the hands on the clock as he had so many times before, and caught a glimpse of himself in a mirror. He beheld a person he did not recognise. He had aged. His face was wrinkled like an old paper bag and his hair grey as smoke. He had shrunk, just like the old woman, and his hands were gnarled and twisted.

It did not take a genius to work out that time had stopped for everyone but himself.

He felt so distraught he took the bead and threw it in the river. Ashamed of his selfishness, he began to help the people who needed his wealth more than he did. To try and put things right, he began leaving parcels of money for the homeless and needy to find.

Nobody knew who the mysterious angel was until quite by chance a little boy saw a bent old man leaving his sick mother one of the now recognisable parcels of wealth. "It's Professor Rich!" the boy yelled for the whole neighbourhood to hear. "He's the one who's been leaving all the money for the poor!"

Now it was all gone. The little boy's mother had had the last parcel. But the news of his outstanding generosity spread, and the little clockmaker became a local celebrity – this time for all the right reasons.

He knew he had to return the clock hands to where they belonged one last time: to take everyone back to a time and a place where "Professor Rich" had never existed and he was what he had always been: Egan Bagley, clockmaker extraordinaire.

In the fullness of time, the Eastgate Clock was mounted in its rightful place above the Eastgate walls of Chester, where it has sat ever since.

Rumour has it that on very rare occasions, the hands on one or more of its faces momentarily and mysteriously… disappear.

The End

Clock Words

See how many clock words you can find...

```
F  A  C  E  T  P  O  D  T  I  C  K  T  O  C  K  A  Z
P  T  C  L  I  U  H  M  T  C  A  A  A  P  O  K  C  J
E  V  I  L  C  L  O  C  K  M  A  K  E  R  D  W  Z  H
N  B  C  M  O  W  G  E  E  M  B  D  P  P  D  Z  W  O
D  T  I  R  E  C  Q  P  F  N  X  J  V  Q  J  J  F  U
U  W  I  G  J  K  K  T  I  M  E  P  I  E  C  E  C  R
L  T  Z  C  B  B  E  S  X  O  C  Z  W  U  I  K  W  G
U  Z  M  O  K  E  L  E  M  H  A  N  D  S  A  I  U  L
M  O  C  Q  H  I  N  V  P  I  N  B  Z  O  Y  K  Q  A
D  I  O  X  E  I  N  T  T  E  T  P  T  W  P  E  S  S
K  O  I  Z  C  N  X  G  N  G  R  H  Q  A  G  P  Z  S
W  E  A  S  T  G  A  T  E  C  L  O  C  K  K  F  U  P
```

Find the following words in the puzzle.
Words are hidden → ↓ and ↘ .

BIG BEN	HANDS	TIMEKEEPER
CLOCKMAKER	HOURGLASS	TIMEPIECE
CLOCKSMITH	PENDULUM	
EASTGATE CLOCK	TICKING	
FACE	TICK-TOCK	

There's nothing to see here. Move on!

Manunitus Sourpuss is a courageous gladiator who is about to fight one of the most feared foes the city has ever encountered.

The Welsh giants have moved in!

But after a number of attempts with his trusty crossbow, he fails to drive the new ogre community away. He receives a gift from an old dear; a bewitched bottle of green mush, a giant antidote. Things are about to change for the people of Deva (the name given to Chester by the Romans). With the temporary magical powers of the gooey substance, the soldier is about to see the giants for who they really are.

It might be a bit scary because they are very tall!

A Very
GIANT TALE

Once upon a time, many years ago when Roman columns looked much posher, there lived a gladiator in an imperial walled city called Deva, in the northwest of England. The lion-hearted man was a courageous soldier with the strength of an ox. He'd participated in many gladiatorial battles in the local amphitheatre, but his latest combat was to be his toughest.

Manunitus Sourpuss was to fight one of the most feared foes the city had ever encountered.

Lampeter Frecklebum

was an...

eno**rm**ous man,

a **GIANT** by any other name. He had moved into the neighbourhood with a tribe of dangerous Welsh giants, who had made their home on nearby land on the other side of the city walls. The plot stepped down towards a gushing river, dug by the hands of the big ones. Fancy columns supported the entrances of their massive sandstone caves, flaunting the magnitude and strength of these unwelcome immigrants.

Frecklebum was the most humongous giant you could have ever met. He was by far the biggest of the new ogre community with a gigantic daylight-obstructing head and the angriest looking face you could ever think of. His hands were like inflated dinghies and his feet like vast boulders.

Shocking to look at, this superhuman was obviously not one to cross, and he, above all others, spread fear and anxiety throughout the city. Each time he was seen, the city dwellers stiffened like frightened rabbits caught in oil lamp lights.

He lifted sandstone slabs the size of elephants and thundered them down with those great hands till they were jammed securely into their final resting places. The Welsh giants had moved in!

Night after night, and more nights after that, Sourpuss lounged in the swish Bridge Street bath house, enjoying the lavish Turkish-style facilities. It was normal for it to be dominated by the Deva gladiators. The leisure complex provided the amenities for him to take his fitness training there, and it was usually when he was having his routine rubdown, he was prone to bragging about his latest successes in battle to his elite fellow officers of The Twentieth Legion.

They had discussed the invasion of the Welsh giants on many occasions at great length: how those big bums were taking diabolical liberties and that. But on this particular night they took a vote. It was time for action.

Sourpuss had clocked up a long service with the legion, with many victories. He had been awarded the most prestigious accolade of all…

CHAMPION!

His comrades decided he was the one to take the fight to the ogres… and what an honour that was.

This was *the* death-defying challenge of all challenges. This was *the* most honourable fight of all fights and he had his trusty crossbow. He could justifiably shoot the Welsh intruders with his crossbow if they stepped within the city walls after night fell and before the sun had a chance to rise. Any other time, he could do nought because the law said so. Of course giants are a law unto themselves, and they brazenly wandered in and out whenever they pleased - just like they owned the place! And who would argue with that?

So for the next six months Sourpuss was out in all weathers training. Hail, the size of lemons, clouted him like sour rocks. He braced the snow in winter and beat the heat in the scorching summer sun, impressing locals. He tossed huge boulders, breaking local records. His muscles grew bulkier by the day.

He practiced several brutal strokes and dazzling movements with a wooden practice sword: thrusting, cutting, and slicing a dangling dummy, thrilling awestruck people who watched on in excitement and amazement at his skills. Many hours of crossbow training made him near perfect. He ran like a deer for miles around the meadows, demonstrating a combination of skills needed to be the top-notch gladiator he was.

The streets were jam-packed with people who had travelled miles to see the champion prepare. Soon, all and sundry were talking about the Gladiator, the one who was going to rid them of those meddlesome giants. He received countless gifts and donations. He had more followers than Justinian Beibussius, The Great Emperor of Entertainment. He also had scores of servants who ran errands everywhere he went. He was now a household name, a killer of all known predators of any size. Many kings had heard of Manunitus Sourpuss.

"SOURPUSS! SOURPUSS! SOURPUSS!"

The chants filled the city as the fever for the Giant Games spread, whooping and whistling every time they saw him.

… Then the great evening arrived. The fearless warrior bound leather cloths around his arms and legs. He strapped a sword belt around his waist, in case things got really nasty. His shoulders were mounted with a metal guard and iron cuisses protected his beefy thighs. His helmet, now glinting from many hours of polishing masked his face. His crossbow had been greased and his arrows sharpened. The Champion was ready…

He shouldered his way through a gully of spectators; all wanting to slap him on his back and wish him well, singing "Glory, Glory, Manunitus!" And when he finally reached the gates, he milked a final farewell cheer by raising a hand and jiggling it around a bit like royalty. This was easier than the fights in the amphitheatre.

Then he finally slipped out through the city gates accompanied by his entourage. He took great positive strides towards the tree he'd chosen which would give him the advantage, not far from the giants' settlement. He proceeded to climb it with the assistance of his servants, bundling and pushing as he went. The servants fled back into the city leaving Sourpuss waiting alone like a solitary leaf wavering on a branch that looked like it was about to snap any minute.

The watchers piled along the city walls with growing excitement, snacking on chickpeas and waiting for the first giant to be slain. In the mocking light of a fire from within Lampeter Frecklebum's abode, the large man himself appeared. He was shadowed by another of his breed, female so they say. At that moment, silence fell as though each person had forgotten how to breathe.

They strode with strides almost as wide as the River Dee and their faces black as thunder. A tense whisper spread across the onlookers as Sourpuss took aim.

They took their first step through the gates of the city walls, at the same time Sourpuss FIRED!

"Ouch!" Frecklebum bellowed.

There were cheers and applause from the walls.

"What's tha matter?" asked the hulking womanlike giant standing next to him. She went by the name of Abergele Smelufeet.

"I've been nipped by somethin', isn't et!" He said in Giant Welsh. He clutched his shoulder like he'd been stung by a bee.

Smelufeet snorted a big giant grunt, expelling a chesty cough. It was a noise she always made when she was tickled pink. "It's one o' them tiny Roman arrows, boyo," she boomed and plucked it out to show him.

Sourpuss fired another bolt from his crossbow which wedged in the ogre's knee. The celebrations heightened as the giant hopped about in discomfort.

"Whose dart is this arrow?" Frecklebum thundered and pinched it out between two clumsy fingers. Through the leaves in a nearby tree he caught sight of movement, Sourpuss crawling along a branch like a cat stuck in a tree.

"**'ERE YOU!**" Frecklebum bellowed, "What are you do-en?!"

Chants of "There's only one Sourpuss!" died down and the crowd waited with baited breath.

Sourpuss was stuck up the tree without a ladder, no servants and then... **SNAP!** His life flashed before his eyes as he plummeted to the ground, bringing with him a collection of leaves, branches and anything else that was living up there. The crowd's participation was of disappointment needless to say. Bruised and confused, he let out a groan, picked up his crossbow and painfully limped back through the city gates, safely away from any retaliation.

Embarrassed and sporting a massive bruised ego as well as a sore bum, he blamed his servants of course and was issued with new ones. On day two he was provided with a much bigger crossbow with lengthier arrows and set off on his second attempt to abolish the ogres from Deva. The crowds gathered once more to wish him well and watch the fun.

Yet again, he left through a valley of well-wishers with chants of encouragement and cheers of expectations; but this time with an undercurrent of jeering. He shinned up the imposing walls and parked himself on top, overlooking the giant's enclosure. Guards pushed back the crowds, catapulting any troublemakers from the area. Servants fussed around him, buffing and polishing anything they possibly could.

Sourpuss was ready. He slid a particularly long arrow from a quiver which had been made deeper. This gave the servants time to dive for cover. He placed it in his enormous crossbow, drew the string back with a bit of a struggle and stood perfectly still.

He must have waited for over an hour or so, standing there like that. His stamina was remarkable. Although a number of watchers had gone home and one or two had brought sleeping cloths and were having a doze. He was therefore startled to feel the numbing grip on his shoulders that he did. How dare they interrupt him when he was on such a vital mission! Where were his servants? He lowered his weapon twisting in a strop, to face, as large as life, Frecklebum! He'd sneaked in without being seen. Surely this was impossible!

"How's et go-en boyo?" The giant cheekily asked as he snatched a bunch of arrows from the quiver and snapped them one by one right under his nose. He had a nerve!

Sourpuss still had one arrow waiting in the wings of his trusty crossbow. There wasn't a moment to squander. He swung the crossbow round; his muscles quivered with the pressure and without further thought, released it with an almighty

TwanG!

By a stroke of luck, it made a beeline for Frecklebum's nostril halting with a stomach-churning crunch.

"**oooOOUCH**!" he bellowed, disturbing every single one of the poor snoozing souls on the walls. "That's just lush, isn't et. Right up my nose!" The big man groaned.

He tried to tug the spear out sending streams of tears down his cheeks. It clearly wasn't going to budge. The watchers fled in all directions now fully awake, and Sourpuss made a hasty retreat, ascending the walls and leaving the giant to deal with his dilemma alone. He wasn't going to stick around.

Back at the baths, Sourpuss took a right ribbing from his colleagues.

"It's not wheel science... just aim and fire." said one.

"I've seen children shoot straighter than that?" said another called Liverpoolius Platypus while loafing in a steamy bath. "Are you actually trying to kill him or are you just playing a game of Tig with him? What are you going to do next, read him a bedtime story?"

Platypus had pleased many on the sands of the amphitheatre and he'd recently been presented with the honour of the yellow scarf which he'd wrapped absurdly around his head. "Let me know when you are ready for me to take over."

The offer would be unthinkable, not to mention downright ill-advised. That buffoon would never be as good as him.

NEVER!

He would show him come rain or shine.

With donations drying up, people's patience running thin and a lack of servants later, the gladiator was about to make his third attempt. It was a dark overcast day when a bent old dear made him a special offer of a bottle of green mush for two chickens. Sourpuss could not see the reason for the sloppy sauce and it smelt of nothing. He didn't dare taste it. It was just as well as the crooked woman told him if he dabbed a decent dollop of the gooey substance on the end of his arrow, she swore the mixture would shrink any giant it hit or his money back with a BOGOF offer thrown in.

What had he got to lose? He accepted the deal and had two chickens beheaded. Fingers crossed the mixture works. The thought of a refund repulsed him. Soon after, he dipped each arrow into the green sticky stuff before placing them in the quiver.

day. To this day, a Roman garden displays the once classical columns which might well have been built by giants. From time to time, giants can be seen parading through the city, and often, an on-guard Roman warrior statue who looks just like Manunitus Sourpuss, can be seen standing perfectly still outside the former bathhouse in Bridge Street where they still sell baked potatoes.

Rumour has it that on rare occasions, you can see his eyes shift as he watches for giants.

The end

Giant Words

See how many giant words you can find…

```
X  K  S  K  S  M  H  U  M  O  N  G  O  U  S  C  M  J
G  I  G  A  N  T  I  C  I  B  Y  N  I  E  V  N  I  X
G  T  F  M  S  B  O  G  R  E  G  M  Z  A  Q  T  G  Z
Y  V  T  O  A  W  E  H  G  J  I  T  A  J  T  I  H  A
I  U  A  N  L  I  M  M  E  N  S  E  I  Y  I  T  T  T
Q  O  D  S  W  G  E  S  W  J  U  M  B  O  N  A  Y  O
Z  X  V  T  T  T  R  E  M  E  N  D  O  U  S  N  Z  S
U  Y  U  R  K  Z  W  Y  I  O  B  D  M  Y  W  I  P  R
K  K  N  O  I  O  L  Y  R  E  C  I  Z  T  W  C  K  C
Z  Z  X  U  P  H  U  G  E  L  K  L  W  C  Z  D  G  C
S  R  L  S  K  P  I  T  D  Z  P  S  D  L  S  U  W  B
A  M  A  S  S  I  V  E  Q  C  S  W  S  E  E  K  I  B
```

Find the following words in the puzzle.
Words are hidden → ↓ and ↘ .

GIGANTIC	MASSIVE	TREMENDOUS
HUGE	MIGHTY	VAST
HUMONGOUS	MONSTROUS	
IMMENSE	OGRE	
JUMBO	TITANIC	

This way to the doll shop...

If you dare!

The Blessington Dolls

For Mum and Dad who brought my dolls to life when I was a child.

Leonard Blessington, owner of the doll shop on Lower Bridge Street, is about to darn something beyond brilliant after a visit from a man in an old claret coat looking like Santa on a bad day!

But by exhibiting the dolls unusual abilities in the Ye Olde Kings Head, the craftsman catches the attention of the locals and news spreads of money to be made. Now, every unscrupulous man and woman in Chester and eventually the whole country want a piece of the fabric!

Now, every unscrupulous man and woman in Chester and eventually the whole country want a piece of the fabric!

This will shock you…

The
BLESSINGTON
DOLLS

Once upon a jolly time when dolls dressed much frillier, there lived a gangling doll maker in an English city where the buildings were the colour of Zebras and the salmon-filled river flowed calmly through its urban land. The lanky man was gifted with a craft needle and about to darn something beyond brilliant.

Indeed, Leonard Blessington's shop was one of the most charming to be seen on the brow of Lower Bridge Street, with only a tiny doll stepping distance away from the River Dee. Dwarfed by its neighbouring buildings, it was thin with ornate guttering and painted bricks – a perfect dolly abode for any sophisticated figurine.

Colour me in

LOWER BRIDGE ST

Three dolls sat comfortably in the Chester shop window, dressed exclusively for them. They could be described as strange looking and not normal. All the dolls in this shop were not conforming to socially accepted customs of style, should we say.

Florence, the one on the left, exhibited cheeks with blobs of red and a circlet of purple hair beneath a fixed turned-back brimmed bonnet with puffed crown. It sat millimetres above her staring eyes. At first glance she looked attractive and la-di-da. Her face seemed to be young and baby-like, yet it was not. It was old in a Victorian sort of way; not timeworn but daubed in middle-aged traits.

Elena, the dark-haired beauty wilting defiantly in the middle, displayed a fascinating expression full of attitude. It was sheer rudeness and only a face a mother could love. Her cheeks gave the impression of a grin but her mouth did not show it and her eyes held a madness of sorts; if that could be possible in a doll of her quality? It was probably the reason why no-one had wanted to buy her, leaving her sagging there like that; dust covered and worn from sun damage.

Finally, with her knitted hood flung back revealing a volcano of red wiry hair was the delightful frowning Isabelle. She pursed her red lips in the most impolite manner and her blown glass eyes were the colour of muddy puddles, too wild to

Cuckoo some would say and it wasn't the ır behaviour you would want one's child to be ıuenced by. She sat to the right of the window.

There was one unique characteristic about each of these plaything's tenderly painted faces who had been made from a hard translucent ceramic material; they looked real as a small child's. But dolls are not like children. Children can laugh and play, dolls can only be played with and be laughed at.

Colour me in

Each day, the monocle wearing craftsman set about sewing features into their flouncy dresses as intricate as the Eastgate Clock's fancy ironwork. He painted personalities onto their pale porcelain faces, of which the likes could never be bought anywhere else. As it happens, the little retail outlet scarcely opened throughout the year, only at the festive time the Victorians love so much.

This time each year, Leonard took public transport and travelled by stage coach from Ramsbottom to Chester. He always stayed at the Ye Olde Kings Head, across the road. He dreamed of travelling in middle-class style and living it up in a posh hotel. The demand for the dolls was so high these days, he worked flat out from dawn till nightfall to meet his deadlines; saving every penny he earned to buy one of those state-of-the-art carts of his own.

The shop was the talk of the city and every little Chester girl wanted to own a 'Blessington Doll'. Not a day went by where a little girl didn't stop with their face pressed against the multi-panelled glazing, gawping in awe at the three eye-catching toys inside the shop. The orders flooded in daily and the stock he'd built over the year had sold out. It was his sheer love of doll making and the need for the finer luxuries in life which urged him to keep sewing.

One cold, late afternoon, when the unspoiled snow had blanketed the pavement outside, the bell rang merrily above the paint peeled door. Expecting to see a mother with her child, he eagerly grabbed his latest masterpiece to show them only to be met with a befuddled looking man. Cloaked in a tatty claret garment and wearing long underpants where his trousers should have been, he looked a lot like Santa but on a bad day. His whiskers were so big and fluffy like feathers, he could have started his own pillow factory. He looked utterly bonkers with it too. Something told Len his visit wasn't going to be a jovial one either.

Thinking he must be a beggar looking for a bit of warmth, his immediate reaction was to tell him, "We're closed," in fear of what he might do.

The fellow merely looked at him, his eyes shifting beneath his tufty brow. "Did you not hear me?" Leonard questioned. He'd met his sort back home and they were not to be trusted. These days in Ramsbottom, you only had to turn your back and someone would nick your Penny Farthing. He told himself not to over-react.

The man had a cheek to smile displaying crooked teeth like a row of crumbling houses. He eventually said:

"Good afterspoon sir.

"That's afternoon," replied Len.

"That's what I said?" the man replied. "I do know that once it goes past three o'clock it isn't the morning anymore."

"You said afterspoon."

"Oh I don't think I did… anyway, those dolls in the window…" he pointed to Florence, Elena and Isabelle. His voice rattled like a noise in a storm, grating and sounding nothing like what St. Nicolas should sound like. "Are they for sale?"

A flat, "No!" was Leonards standard answer to that question. "You can place an order and I will make a similar doll for you. All my dolls are unique so they won't be exactly like those."

"Why are they so special to you? Surely you can sell them to a fellow dolliteer?" The man asked - curt in his response. He was exactly a foot smaller than Leonard so shouldn't really have been a threat. "I'm not one to put all my eggs in one mixing bowl, but I'm willing to pay good money to have them all now. Can't you replace them?" He sounded too insistent for the shop owner's liking.

"I think you mean basket." Leonard eyed the man. A haircut and a shave would improve his appearance no end. He says he has money and yet looks so shabby and talks so confused.

Santa shook his head not understanding.

"It should be: put all eggs in one basket." continued Leonard. He grunted then tenderly laid the precious doll in his hands onto the counter, taking care to plump her dress and to neatly arrange her hair. "They can't be replaced. They were the ones my father made – they are NOT for sale."

"I see." The man considered leaving. He ran a knobbly hand through his hair and Leonard imagined his fingers would get stuck any minute. Nearly looking away in embarrassment at the forthcoming entanglement Leonard saw the man free his hand and step towards the window. He looked back at the doll lying on the counter. "You have your father's gift," he complimented him and then reached for a window doll before asking, "May I?"

Leonard gave an uncertain nod as the guest picked each doll up in turn; grasping their tiny hands and making them stand. He seemed respectful.

"Why did your father not paint smiles on their faces?" he examined. No-one had ever asked this before.

"Some he did, those he didn't," the doll maker said. "If you want smiles, I will paint smiles."

The stranger placed the last doll back on its seat and strode over to the counter. He stretched across the counter clasping Leonard's hands without delay. It was unexpected and unusual. He flinched. His eyes widened and his monocle slipped away.

"A gift like yours should be blessed Mr Blessington." It was an ironic thing to say. Were his hands not already blessed?

Leonard couldn't tell if his tone was sincere but he was taken aback nevertheless. The man's hands held a strange heat which seared through his whole body. The last time he had felt like that was when he found out he had to pay for the next round at the pub. The man then left without another word and without ordering a doll!

Leonard scratched his pink balding head then threw on a hat and overcoat and locked the door for the night. He hurried across the road, to his local haunt, the Ye Olde Kings Head. It was his favourite place to lodge. He told some of the punters about his mysterious visitor.

"That's Stinky Joe," said George, one of the regulars. "I'm surprised you don't know of him. He smells of wee. He was never the same since he slipped on that banana skin and he took to tying his drawers round his head. Barmy he is. Mind you, I haven't seen him for years. He's known for his…strange ways should I say."

"Old Joseph reckons he can do magic," chipped in the portly one at the end of the bar. "He's nothing more than a scrounger - begging all the while. A weasel."

"He didn't beg from me," added Leonard, taking a generous slurp from his pint of bitter allowing some to dribble down his chin in his haste. It was a treat he deserved. "…and he was wearing his underpants in the right place when I saw him."

"How do you know?" George asked.

"Well he had no trousers on so I could see them."

"Told you," laughed George. "Barmy."

"…and he offered to buy my three dolls in the window as it happens."

"Don't know where he would have got the money for your dolls, Len – he wasn't going to buy them - more like steal them." The large man butted in once again.

"You listen to me," George cut in suddenly serious. He took a firm hold of Leonard's arm. "You watch out for old Joseph…" he paused dramatically. "He's not someone to mess with. He can make impossible things happen." It was the drink talking – either that or he listens to too many urban legends.

At the crack of dawn, Leonard returned back to his little shop stooping his way through the doorway, going about his business as he always did, dusting and winding the music boxes high on the shelf behind the counter. They were one of his best sellers and he had to make certain they played on demand for the next little girl to walk in with a head full of ballet and fairy-tales. It provided that magical shopping experience they sought.

It was then when he heard a mysterious scratching sound, like a scuffle over by the window. He snapped the music box shut and all went silent. Dratted mice! He would have to check if he had a spare trap later.

He shrugged and thought no more of it. This was a huge mistake because mice like these could cause serious damage to dolls like them. He lifted the lid but over the music he heard a faint pattering. When he closed the cover, it stopped. He lurched towards the noise to see his dolls, Florence, Elena and Isabelle staring out of the frozen window in their usual positions with an equally chilly stare. For a moment he thought Isabelle had shifted along her seat but he couldn't be sure.

"Rats!" He would need a large snare if it were.

He would check in a minute. He continued working, music chiming around him when a patter, a rattle then clomping of sorts overpowered the room.

Snap!

The music stopped instantly. He grabbed some old cloth and hurtled towards the window to catch the pest but stopped right away because of what he saw. It was impossible! Improbable! It was perhaps against the law of saneness. Clever rats! All three dolls had been - rearranged! He searched but there wasn't a long-tailed rodent in sight.

Then something occurred to him. He was probably being silly. Still, no-one else was here, just him - so who would know what he was thinking? He turned his back to the window and with the music box still in his hand, he lifted the lid.

It started with a faint tapping which flourished into a jumble of thuds and clunks as the music got going. The sounds had some weight to them - like small people. Len went cold… and it wasn't because of the draft whistling through the crack in the window frame, but a flow of realisation. A downright freezing one at that.

Leaving the music playing he mustered up the courage to face the sounds. It was not two or four, but six sets of steps he heard and there they were. His three beloved dolls danced like puppets without strings. They bopped like no-one watched and to Ding Dong Merrily on High!

Out popped Leonard's eyeglass. It was a good job it was virtually shatter proof. He snapped the box shut and the dolls collapsed to their seats like a game of musical chairs. His eyes were wide, his mouth dry and his face whitened like a mountain in a blizzard. It can't be happening! He was over-worked. He needed a rest!

But that day he stitched and painted as fast as his tired hands would allow. It was as though he'd forgotten what had happened that morning. Of course he hadn't. When he finished the last doll, he threw an uncertain glance at the music box. Before he could think he'd grabbed it, opened it and the music played. Ding Dong Merrily on High tinkled prettily as before, bringing five new dolls to life.

They danced on top of his counter accompanied by the dolls in the window. It had to be a miracle! Leonard could hardly believe his widened eyes which left his right eye bare once again. It seemed that each new doll he'd created with those blessed hands of his, conjured an enchanted dancing puppet.

That night he carefully wrapped his father's dolls and placed them in a cloth bag. He then rushed across to the pub.

"Watch!" he said after telling the spectators about the phenomenon. He lined them on the table, and opened the Christmas box. The melody dinged once again from the small container and sure enough, the dolls danced. The punters were astounded.

"It must be some type of high-tech device like clockwork or something," said George holding his

cut glass tumbler in the air and checking his drink for something foreign in it.

"No it isn't, George," Leonard informed him. "I tell you... it was Joseph. He put a spell on my dolls and on my hands, too. So every doll I make can dance. It surely is a wonderful miracle."

News spread until everyone in the city had heard about the miracle and every Tom, Dick, and Harry wanted to own a Blessington Doll. It was Tom, Dick, and Harry and every other man and woman in the city who could see a fortune to be had as well.

The very next day, Leonard's shop window darkened. He heard a number of excited voices outside the window and opened his door to be faced with a large crowd waiting to see him.

He took their orders and worked through the night. Each morning he would appear bleary eyed in the little shop doorway. Every day was the same. His window would darken and the voices would start. They would also spend hours chanting words like:

"What do we want?"

"Dolls!"

"When do we want them?"

"Now!" They would shout.

And:

"There's only one Len Blessington! There's only one Blessington!"
He grew sick of hearing his own name and begged them to stop.

Not only that, evenings were spent entertaining multitudes of people at the Ye Olde Kings Head. News spread and people travelled miles to get a look at the spectacle. Leonard became rich beyond his dreams but he could never stop working to enjoy it, as much as he wanted to. They were his dolls but the problem was, his customers: Tom, Dick, and Harry and the rest of the crowd had shillings in their eyes and they too were now well-off but wanted more.

"I'm sorry," he croaked one morning as he emerged from his shop, too weary. Buyers woke from their sleeping bags and makeshift tents. The street was jam-packed with them. They would be waiting anywhere there was a space: a step, a pavements, a doorway, his doorway! Leonard didn't know what they'd suffered just to get their hands on one of those money making dolls… and then he told them:

"I'm not taking any more orders."

His words hit silence. They weren't fully awake. It was open to question whether he had chosen the

85

right time to release this bit of information because if they weren't morning people they could take this somewhat badly.

"Please tell everyone, I'm not taking any more orders!" he called out and slammed the door, locking and bolting it behind him. This did the situation no favours and it was then it was confirmed, they were not good-natured at daybreak!

First the hammering started, then the shouting – all desperate for one of those dolls. The anger grew and Leonard had taken to working upstairs, never opening his doors in fear of what the people would do.

In the early hours, he smuggled his precious Florence, Elena and Isabelle, creeping through the abundance of sleeping folk to the public house across the road. After a few attempts of waking the Landlord and trying not to wake the protestors, he was let in. The proprietor of the inn could see Leonards plight and of course, now being made a wealthy man from the money Leonard had drawn in, he helped him hide the dolls in his room.

Dolls like those were not still for long. Night after night, they would dance to any music they heard: tapping, striding and stomping around the public house. But he couldn't risk them being stolen so he stopped the shows and locked them out of sight.

The two hundred and fifty dolls he had made were shown around the country with owners becoming rich beyond their wildest dreams and soon everyone wanted one. They were demanded every time they saw him and some people were so obnoxious, Leonard actually feared for his life. Greed had taken over.

Things were so bad that terror had spread amongst the little girls who used to long for one of those frilly little playthings. Instead, it would give them the collywobbles and they would tremble at the mere sight of the doll shop.

The next morning was the day when the man who started this pandemonium but for whom little was known walked in. Leonard knew it was him because he smelt him first.

"Joseph!" the shop-keeper called out. His visit was unexpected but this time welcomed. "I am so pleased to see you."

"Good after-jelly-spoon," replied Joseph. Leonard choose not to correct him this time. He said, "It's the charm you put on my dolls and myself, it was a blessing at first but now, everyone wants a doll and everyone wants to see them dance. I can't cope with it you see."

"What charm?" Joseph asked looking totally confused.

Leonard ignored his question. "Everybody is getting greedy. They are all becoming so rich they want more and it's become a curse."

"Curses, purses, it's all a bunch of rubbidish, nonsensical codswollop. Who needs money?"
He nearly left Leonard lost for words but he managed a: "We all do."

"I know it's your bed and butter but how much butter do you want with it?

"I think you mean bread…" the tall man replied.

"Allow me to be point with you Mr Blessington…" bellowed Joseph so loudly it startled Leonard.

"I think that should be blunt…" Leonard pointed out. He didn't know why he even bothered.

"I offered to buy your father's dolls…" He looked shifty. "Give me them dolls and I will help you with that, what do you call it? Thingamapig…" he stopped and sniggered. "Oh yes a charm, and peace and hostility will be restored across Chester and indeed across the country."

"I – I – I can't…!" Len looked visibly shocked. " No! No! Absolutely not! Out of the question!" He shook his head. This was outrageous!

"Then I'm afraid I can't help you," the vagrant turned towards the door.

"Stop!" Len had no choice. He couldn't let this hell go on. "I will get you the dolls – after you lift the spell." His stomach did a hundred and one somersaults at the thought of losing his precious figurines.

"I might be able to assist you with removing this er…" he coughed, "smoke of bad luck you've been having but it would be unlikely to be able to do this with dolls. It would be out of the question. You're asking too much of me."

"But we can't let the dolls continue with these capabilities. It's making everyone greedy and violent. Seeing you were the one who…" he daren't say it, "…made this happen."

"Are you suggesting I have supernormal abilities? I'm not a saucer," Joseph's eyebrows arched. "You were the one who made the dolls."

A bead of sweet rolled down Leonard's brow. He hadn't thought of him as a sorcerer. For crying out loud, the man didn't even know the right words but at this moment he hoped he was. He must be. He had to be!

"I made my dolls the way I always make them. So why can they now dance?" That was a good question.

"You are right my man. This self-indullness can't go on like this," the old man reasoned. "The dolls can't have the bad luck removed from them, but they will have to be got rid of," he told him. "…for good, for never and never."

Len's heart sank. His beautifully hand crafted dolls had to be destroyed. It didn't bare thinking about. All his hard work. Not only that, it will cause mayhem across the country. These people would never give up their beloved money making machines.

"How can I get them back to Chester? The people will protest."

"I can get them back," said the bearded man confidently. "I sir, will ensure I get every single little frilly doll back to Chester."

The man was a lunatic. "They will kill you!" Leonard now feared for the tramp. "How can you possibly get these living dolls away from these reprobates?"

"Don't worry about those gigglemugs. Asking me about dolls is like asking Penny if she knows anything about farthings," replied Joseph.

"Standing in a doll shop doesn't make you an expert any more than standing in a stable makes you a horse," responded Leonard. He frowned. If Stinky Joe can talk nonsense, then so could he.

"Yes but you can't lead a horse to water but you can make him drink it," said Joseph gripping the doll maker's hands and chanting some strange words. He then said, " I need some of those music boxes."

Night fell and in the early hours Twinkle Twinkle Little Star could be heard tinkling around the city Rows as well as Silent Night and a concoction of other tunes. Joseph rushed around the city winding each box over and over again and he did so every single night.

Meanwhile, Leonard had to convince the angry crowds he did not have the gift anymore and made them dolls which did not dance to prove it. The crowds disappeared over the next couple of months.

One evening, while shutting his shop up for the night, Leonard caught sight of Joseph placing the music boxes around the area like he did every evening for the last six months. He felt sorry for the man, suspecting he had turned more nuttier than he already was. The poor soul still believed he could rid the country of dolls. With saddened eyes, Leonard lowered his head and walked away.

The old man scurried around winding boxes which were now battered and manky. With that sort of mankiness it was a wonder they still played. He danced about the street to the tinkling music in the middle of the horrid comments people would make as they passed by. He would chase them out of his way shouting words which didn't make sense.

Another evening when Leonard had locked his shop up for the night, he spotted Joseph hopping around at the top of the street. He wasn't sure why but he watched for a few minutes intrigued at what the man was doing.

Tonight was no different. He span round nearly falling over then hopped in a number of directions like he always did. While clapping and flapping his arms around like a mad man, he sang words that meant nothing. He rushed over to the music boxes when they stopped playing and wound them over and over again. He continued his routine. He was obviously a man who never gives up.

Leonard turned to cross the road. His pint was calling him but it was a tapping and clattering in the distance which made him stop. He glanced back up to the top of the street to see Joseph now rushing as fast as his bent old legs would allow, clambering the steps up into the Rows above the shops.

Leonard decided to follow. At first he walked. Then his pace quickened. His heart pounded. He recognised that sound and found himself running. It grew louder the nearer he drew. He entered Bridge Street and was met with a deafening hammering sound.

"Well blow me down with an ear trumpet!" Leonard hadn't seen anything like this before. If it wasn't his dancing dolls! Like rows of pegs on a washing line, the banisters were filled with them – two hundred and fifty of them to be exact!

Joseph held his arms up in warm approval, clapping and dancing at the same time. Leonard spotted Joseph climbing down to street level just by a stone pillared cross. He held a music box and the dolls followed him. They seemed different, almost stronger. Their bodies and arms were stationary but they moved with rapid leg and foot movements.

Joseph waited. Then he counted them. When he was happy, he marched. Every now and again he turned back to face the dolls and tried to dance like them, nearly losing his balance. Leonard waited in a doorway as they rumbled past.

The beating of their feet thundered down Lower Bridge Street, under a bridge and along the River banks. The shop keeper trailed behind. Just past the bandstand loomed a large suspension bridge framing the darkened flowing river. Leonard hid inside the platform and watched through the rails.

Normally delightful to be around, the river felt unwelcoming. Close by was something floating in the water. It bobbed against the river's edge attached by rope to a wooden post. Every now and again it would disappear under the surface. It had been bobbing around there for six months. Joseph had tied it there in preparation.

It took six long months of organisation: the winding, the music, the dancing, the travelling... who knew what these dolls had gone through to get here?

The bobbing thing in the river was pulled back to the edge. It was a rotten piece of wood. The dolls thundered their feet behind him like mechanical devices. He carefully placed the music box which had seen better days, on top of the wood, winding it as he did. It was one of Leonards best sellers. It displayed a striking decorated red and black pattern on the outer case, hand-painted by the craftsman himself.

The tune was appropriate: Twinkle, Twinkle Little Star. The chiming sound evaporated into the night sky. It sounded eerie. It was then Joseph chose to release the rope and push the decayed wood towards the middle of the river.

Leonard gulped. This was the moment. It took him two long days to make one of those dolls. That was over four thousand hours of work and now his dolls would be lost forever, at the bottom of a river. It was a small price to pay for peace and hostility!

The two hundred and fifty dolls stamped their right feet on the ground, hopping, then treble tapping their left feet. Cutting their left feet towards their right hips, they box stepped their way down the bank. It was a fabulous parade. People would pay good money to watch this.

Joseph waved his arms to the tune tickling from the music box which faded as it floated away. The dolls past him tapping and box stepping until unaccountably, one by one, they fell in, each and every single one of them. Then there was silence.

The very next morning Len shouldered his way through hordes of confused and angry local folk. They had been waiting outside the doll shop demanding to know where their dolls had gone to. He explained they had last been seen dancing towards the river and then escaped inside the premises. It was then Joseph returned for his payment.

Begrudgingly, Len handed the cloth bag which held the carefully wrapped dolls.

"Take care of my father's dolls won't you," Len instructed with a tear in his eye and turned away. They were the only remaining dolls which could still dance. Joseph saw the tear. He was impressed the man would give up something so precious in order to rid the world of selfishness. He took the dolls out of the bag and went straight over to the window. He placed Florence, Elena and Isabelle in their seats where they belonged and then said, "Farewell until we meet a hen," before he left.

The city soon returned back to normal. The doll maker was extra careful not to let anyone see the dolls dance ever again. The ex-doll-owners soon moved on from their selfishness and strangely forgot about the dancing dolls and Joseph, he was last seen with his underpants tied round his head, dancing towards the river. He was never to be seen again.

To this day, the shop still displays dolls but if they can dance or not is anyone's guess. Gossip has it, that every now and then, the pitter-patter of dolls dancing feet can still be heard in the room Leonard use to stay in at the Ye Olde Kings Head and sometimes, music can be heard tinkling from a music box on Bridge Street Rows.

The end

Smelly words
See how many smelly words you can find...

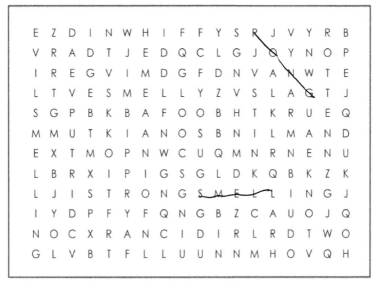

Find the following words in the puzzle.
Words are hidden → ↓ and ↘ .

EVIL-SMELLING
FOUL
PONG
PUTRID
RANCID

RANK
REEKING
ROTTEN
SMELLY
STINK

STRONG-SMELLING
WHIFFY

This way

An Imp Called Boo

Dedicated to Caiden

You might need a magnifying glass because this guy is tiny!

An Imp
CALLED BOO

.

Once upon a time when imps looked much smaller, there lived a mischievous imaginary being called Boo. Branded as 'The Chester Imp' he occupied a space high up on the north nave wall of the ancient walled city's glorious cathedral. Since a monk had been half scared to death by a demonic face at one of the nave windows, Boo's job was to sit there in order to frighten away any leering demons. Unfortunately, he was such a good looking specimen so much so, each day and night he spent many hours sat high up at the window staring at his own reflection.

On the few occasions when the little creature left the window side he loved nothing more than to blow his own trumpet and speak of his good looks to the other grotesques and mystical creatures that lurked within the grounds. Each time, his self-imageries sounded more outlandish and incredible.

At Christmas, he told an enchanted window image that his eyes held a sparkle as bright as the holy star and insisted she looked. She was so furious at his self-perception she blew out the candles by her side so she didn't have to look at him anymore. He foolishly believed it was because he out-shone them.

On Valentine's Day, Boo told the haughty angels he was a gift from god. One shot an arrow at him in anger and he stupidly thought it had been sent from cupid.

On Shrove Tuesday, the conceited pint-sized imp told a snooty lord he was so good looking that he did not look like a creature with any sins and therefore did not have any. The snooty lord scoffed at his naivety and called him "A Pancake." Boo was so pleased with this honour, he told everyone to call him the same.

By wintertime, the cathedral's creatures were so fed up with calling him a pancake and with the self-admiring rascal in general; they wanted to teach him a lesson but did not know how. A no-nonsense gargoyle king heard the whispers and decided enough was enough and the trifling nincompoop should not be mollycoddled any more. He found Boo and told him that he should speak no more of his good looks. Boo demanded it was part of his job.

After uttering a few magical words, the king said, "You shall sit at the nave window but if you want to keep your good looks, never behold your reflection. If you do, you will grow to be a truly hideous looking creature and then you will turn to stone and will be hard to see forever."

"But I don't want to become hard to see forever...or hideous!" Boo protested. He expected to be the centre of attention.

The king raised her hand to silence him. "Boo, this is the only way your self- appreciation will ever be respected as you will then do the job you are here to do."

Boo pooh-poohed this but returned to his normal place and tried for a whole five minutes not to look at his reflection but could not help himself, his image looked so handsome. He frowned at his own self-indulgence and without further ado he grew hideous and turned into an ugly stone carving.

To this day, the devil has not ever dared to look in the cathedral and despite being repulsive; Boo is one of the most respected stone carvings in the cathedral.

Rumour has it; if you are able to see him, you might catch him staring at his own reflection in the glass.

The end

Tiny Words
See how many tiny words you can find...

```
G N X P D Y F S V N A G T T O I P P
X T G P K N E E H I G H Z C S H E O
J B T E U M I C R O S C O P I C E C
Z H V J Y R R I F U N S I Z E X W K
L I D D U V X K D P D T E E N Y E E
S S J U N Q C F R T U G Y T M D E T
M P E T I T E P M I N U S C U L E S
H I T T Y B I T T Y A W C E U G N I
D M B I W R J X U F G F B S V I K Z
T R I N S I G N I F I C A N T C B E
P M I N I S J Z J L I T T L E F H D
O S G T P H P V R G O B M U K G T H
```

Find the following words in the puzzle.
Words are hidden → ↓ and ↘ .

FUN-SIZE
INSIGNIFICANT
ITTY-BITTY
KNEE-HIGH
LITTLE

MICROSCOPIC
MINI
MINUSCULE
PEEWEE
PETITE

POCKET-SIZED
TEENY

112

Get ready…

for the **biggest**...

stink of your life…

118

Flip the page...

Colour me in

Waft the smell...

Pooooooh!

Hodgepodge

Dedicated to Kyla

This light-fingered goblin would sell anything if he could. Even the clothes off his grandmother's back!

Despite this, he has a very important job to do: to guard the Anglo-Saxon coins passed down by his thieving ancestors, which hold a magical healing power.

After John Pemberton takes over Goblin Tower as his base for his new rope business, the stinking gnome of a man uses practical jokes and this superpower for his own ill-gotten gains. He is now in serious trouble with the Folklore Association!

Hodgepodge

Once upon a smelly time, there lived a Goblin who stunk of trump, wee and sweaty feet. The kindest way to describe the sprite in this story would be 'a hoarder.' But if you were being truthful, he was a notorious thief whose tomfooleries did nothing else but upset and cause a lot of trouble for his victims. His horrendous stash of bits and pieces stunk of something beyond foul; generally, the contents of a bucket thrown from an upstairs window. This smelly being maybe tiny but he was head and shoulders above all others when it came to mischief and stealing. You certainly would never buy a used packhorse from this guy as it was more than likely it would have been stolen or have dodgy parts.

This reprobate goes by the name of

Hodgepodge.

Hodgepodge wasn't ashamed of his social class. The revolting squatter happily renamed his medieval abode, 'Goblin Tower'. The circular medieval tower sat astride the age-old city walls of Chester in the North West of England with an exclusive gated entrance and stunning views. It was here he had lived all his life, rent free, and it was here he felt like a king. But he was here for a legitimate ancient reason: to guard the Anglo-Saxon coins which had been passed down by his thieving ancestors. The coins were hidden in a secret underground store beneath the tower's floor.

The cellar space was enough for someone of Hodgepodge's build which was in proportion to a medium-sized pig. Funny enough, he had big floppy ears, and if his large leathery nose were flatter, he would unquestionably look like a pig.

He had a great sense of smell due to the size of his nostrils and had this incredible ability to sniff and root out food despite the overpowering smell he emitted from himself. He was able to move sufficiently around this confined space which spanned the whole width of the upper floor. He could hide out and lay low for days when something big had gone down. He kept supplies of food and drink here and had a special place to wee and poo (which he never emptied). It was self-emptying if you like. It either seeped out through the gaps at the bottom of the compartment or dried up and decomposed itself over time and left a disgusting odour.

The one hundred and twenty-two coins held a healing power which would not work if they fell into non-goblin hands. The Folklore Association had regrettably found out about them back in 1694 and six years later, the by-law they had enforced to control their usage and safeguard their secret, remained. It stipulated that Goblin Tower should always have a resident warden from the goblin race in return for this rent-free accommodation, the afore mentioned goblin would heal any Chester citizen in need of it by pressing one of the coins against his or her flesh which would heal the most debilitating illness. In human hands it would be worth nothing more than chocolate money. So, the jammy rascal did not actually have to pay for anything as what he did not have given to him by the law, he just helped himself to anyway. But even though the coins were rightfully his, the Hobgoblin could never be allowed to spend them to his disappointment. This light-fingered goblin would sell anything if he could, even the clothes off his grandmother's back, so it was a good job. At least there were some perks to the job: he would never become sick, not even a cough. But he takes these powers for granted and does not appreciate what he has, which is something that money cannot buy.

Each day, the little man would set out, scurrying along the city walls, deceiving, and robbing and stinking all the places out. The days would be overshadowed by this deceit and the mischievous pranks. He would return with his loot, proud of every hoard, hated by many. If it was shiny, he had to have it and if it wasn't nailed down, he took it. It all added to his assortment of odds and sods. So much so, it was getting to the point he could hardly move around the tower for the lack of space these days.

He had a saying:

"What you see is what you get."

Then, one cold day, Hodgepodge returned from a grueling day of pilfering with his hood clenched tightly around his uncombed tufts, hot footing his way along the city's roman walls. He had wet his pants several times since he didn't have time to find a place to go. He did not care. He was too busy for mundane things like personal hygiene. This was about the fifth day this week he had done this, and he didn't even bother to change his clothes. Who would complain since he lived in the tower alone? Anyway, this day he had upset one local too many and it wasn't just because of the foul smell. He had to make a quick get-a-way only to find his tower had been invaded! How was he going to explain this one to the F.A.? He immediately hid and observed.

It was **barbaric!**

Men rooted through his collection of rubbish, throwing it into a pile to burn or recycle. Moving his things from their usual places was not a good thing. Hodgepodge could not breath and felt a panic attack looming. Luckily, the shiny things he classed as valuable, were hidden with the coins under the floor. Didn't they know the tower was protected under goblin law? They had no rights. They scrubbed and fumigated his living quarters.

More men rallied around beneath the walls in an opening at ground level under the tower. It was packed with yarn and huge containers full of gooey tar. It smelt very nearly as bad as Hodgepodge's quarters. Some of the men felt sick and had to peg their noses or wrap scarves round their faces to cover their mouths and noses. They were overcome with tar and smells of Hodgepodge. Once the large iron gates were locked, they left. The pot-bellied goblin took the opportunity and sped into the tower. With a struggle, he squeezed into the space under the floor where his shiny loot remained. From now on, he would have to live in these small boundaries amongst the pots and pans and drinking vessels he had classed as precious and see who the new occupants were. Then he would introduce himself.

The next morning broke with a distinct sound of voices. Hodgepodge bravely pushed the large sandstone boulder he had cunningly wedged over the hole where he hid. He popped his head out. It was safe. He crept out of the tower and peeped below. A group of men were running back and too, unravelling twines and threads of yarn and fixing them to a large wheel device some distance away across the grove below.

"John Pemberton!" A voice called. Hodgepodge ducked. "How's the ropewalk coming along?" Two men approached and greeted each other. John Pemberton was a respectable member of the community, the mayor of Chester no less and now a proprietor of a rope making business.

"All set sir. We shall have our first order complete by the end of the week."

The little podgy onlooker had shillings in his eyes. "What you see is what you get," he whispered to himself before scuttling away.

The next day, John Pemberton had entered the tower where he sat all day, watching over his workers below. He did not trust his workers to put all their energy into it, so he gestured to them from his tower to make sure they weren't idle and booted anyone out who appeared work shy!

Hodgepodge had been out early on his rounds not expecting to see him there. Pemberton had a comfortable chair brought in and facilities had been arranged for his own personal refreshment to make this amount of sitting a tad easier on him while his men and even some children sweated below.

The man grumbled a lot and shouted frequently at his workers to move faster. He had deadlines to meet and more ships were coming in and they expected rope. Hodgepodge decided now was a good time for introductions. Pemberton jumped at the sight of him and instantly stood up from the security of his armchair. The fright had left him a little shaken for a moment.

"What are you doing in Pemberton's Parlour?" The Mayor asked sternly. He felt fairly chuffed with the new name of the tower he'd just conjured up over a cuppa but didn't show it.

Pemberton's Parlour! Hodgepodge could not

believe what he was hearing. How dare he! He composed himself then said, "Hodgepodge, Sir." He held out a reasonably clean hand, apart from a few poo stains and a bit of soil.

"I beg your pardon?" The Mayor flinched. He shied away from the goblin's dirty hand. The smell had put him off. "You have no business being here!"

"My name, it's Hodgepodge. I am honoured to meet you sir. I have come to offer my services and can 'elp you spin your yarn into rope. All I ask for in return is food and a few cups of that delicious tea of yours." He used his poshest voice in the hope he would appear professional.

Pemberton desperately wanted to meet his deadlines and an extra pair of hands would be appreciated clean or not, and at hardly any cost so he agreed. The next day, Hodgepodge worked all day and into the early evening spinning rope, only stopping for a bit of food and a brew or two. At the end of the day, his pile of rope was the highest. The owner could plainly see how productive the little creature was at little cost to him so was satisfied he had got the best end of the deal.

That night, Hodgepodge could not help himself. It was in a goblins nature to play practical jokes. It wasn't his best prank, but he thought it would be amusing to replace the Mayor's sugar for salt and laughed so much he nearly wet himself. He couldn't imagine anything funnier than what the look on the Mayor's face would be like when he tasted it.

The next morning, Hodgepodge prised himself from under the floorboards and discreetly entered the mayor's office like he had just come from somewhere else. He had come to offer his services once again and in the nick of time too. The Mayor took a mouthful of tea when he entered much to Hodgepodges delight, then spat it out, chucking the rest of the cup's contents out of the tower onto his workers below. The man was furious and took a while to sort himself out while Hodgepodge struggled painfully to contain his laughter.

This time Hodgepodge did not want to drink the Mayor's tea or eat his food, especially now it had been tampered with. Instead, he asked for one of the Mayors fancy and hopefully embroidered jackets as payment. The fact the Mayor was six foot two and the little urchin was three foot nothing did not bother him. The jacket would clearly drown the little sow of a goblin, but it would hide his wet pants when necessary. The Mayor had hundreds of jackets and for him it was money for old rope so to speak. He agreed urging him to get to work.

And work he did. Hodgepodge worked all day and into the early evening, hardly stopping at all. He worked wonders with building stockpiles and supported the slow ones who could tolerate him being near them. Pemberton took notice and despite the stench, he knew this foolish being was worth having around. To keep him happy, he took off the jacket he wore that day and gave it to him. Hodgepodge pranced around wearing it like he was a king as it trailed behind him like a cloak. His employer laughed at his stupidity.

"What would you like tomorrow?" he asked. "A sock? I could maybe stretch to a pair," he mocked. Hodgepodge merely laughed along with him.

That night, when everyone had gone home, Hodgepodge broke into the store and stole the rope he and the others had spent all day making and tied together the horse cartwheels of all the carts used to transport the stock to the buyers. It took most of the night twisting Reef knots, rolling Hitches, looping Figure-Eight knots and coiling Bowlines. There were so many. His rope talents were exceptional and never ending and gave him hours of laughter and entertainment. This has got to be one of his best pranks ever. He had excelled himself this time.

The next day, Pemberton grew so angry when he found the carts roped together like that and blew his top. With fists clenched and his face glowing like a lantern, he yelled:

"Undo it, undo it all…
NOW!"

Tools were thrown and buckets were kicked in a temper. The rope crew cowered in fear of being picked to sort this mess out. The goblin's shenanigans had done such a superb job of costing Mayor Pemberton hours of worker's pay to get it un-roped. The first deadline was approaching, meaning all his men had to work without pay all that night. The day and night brought Hodgepodge hours of happiness as he spent most of his time battling to contain his laughter. The Mayor was beginning to dislike the creature more than ever and noticing that Hodgepodge seemed so knowledgeable in helping the men unravel some of the knots, he couldn't help but wonder if he had something to do with it.

Soon, some of the over-worked men who were so sick with heat, exhaustion and dehydration started to collapse. Not realising he was one of the underlying causes for making the men work harder, Hodgepodge felt pity for them and decided he should bring out one of the healing coins from under the tower's floor and make them better again. One by one, he discretely closed the sick workers hands around the coin for one minute. By a small miracle, they felt better again.

Unbeknown to Hodgepodge, John Pemberton witnessed the goblin with his own eyes. Amazed by what seemed to be healing hands, he knew he had to keep the goblin on his payroll whatever it took... shoelaces, scarves, ties, he could have whatever he wanted. He clearly was an asset to the company.

Funny enough, the following week, the Mayor turned up to Pemberton's Parlour five minutes later than usual, shivering, coughing and spluttering all over the place. The man was a complete mess. He demanded to see Hodgepodge. This time he would allow the goblin's unclean hands to touch him, to make him better. He even removed the silken scarf he usually used to cover his mouth and nose when in his vicinity, mainly because he'd lost his sense of smell.

"Hodgepodge!" he sputtered and coughed. "I've seen you do it, make me better." He dropped dramatically to the floor, unable to pull himself up.

The little man had to give this some serious thought and took some time over it while the man choked in front of him. What was in it for him?

"Hodgepodge!" the sick man croaked.

The goblin eventually agreed, "I will heal you sir, but in return you must tell me where you think I live, or you will have to give the rope business to me."

The sick man choked even more at the thought. "This isn't time for games!" he managed to wheeze. "Get me better!"

Hodgepodge did not like his tone but still, he couldn't see the man suffer like that. He carefully placed the Anglo-Saxon coin in the Mayor's hand without him seeing for one minute, and then he felt completely better. The Mayor did not see it happen, he did not feel it happen, and he did not know how it could have happened…but it did and he didn't care how, as long as he was better.

"Thank you, thank you!" It was a miracle! The mayor sounded grateful for a change.

He scrambled to his feet and sat on his chair mopping his brow with his silken scarf and then placed it over his face. He could smell Hodgepodge again. He would never have imagined he would be as pleased as he was to smell him again.

"Let me know what you would like – my narrow-brimmed silk top hat, a flared frock-coat…" Pemberton had upgraded his payments to him in line with what he thought his services were worth.

"You have to guess Mr. Pemberton, or the ropewalk will belong to me," said the little bandit, letting him know exactly what he wanted.

"Or, or," the man stuttered, "you could have my favourite waistcoat with the high upstanding collar. You would look stylish in that."

Hodgepodge shook his head.

Pemberton was so worried by the Goblin's powers. He made one last attempt to persuade him.

"I, I, I can give you a permanent job, a, a, a, job for life!" pleaded the Mayor. "You could live here in the store shed with your own hand-crafted chamber pot and a clean jug of water every single night."

The man had selfish reasons to keep the goblin there for the rest of his life; he needed him to heal him each time he was sick.

"You would have to clean yourself up of course," he added. "We couldn't have the rope smelling of something you'd trodden in."

Hodgepodge thought it sounded lavish but luxuries like that did not appeal to him because it just wasn't enough. He wanted more.

"I will give you a total of five guesses and five guesses only Mayor Pemberton, so use them wisely,"

"And what if I don't?" the man asked.

"Then a terrible curse will befall on your establishment pronounced by the supernatural spiritual power of the Folklore Association and will last…" he paused dramatically, his eyes widened, a bead of sweat rolled down the side of his face (not because of fear but because he was hot) then he said, **"FOREVER"** in a silly deep voice.

This was not true of course. Hodgepodge had made it all up. He had once overheard a drunken gypsy cursing a local Cestrian (a resident of, or person from, the city of Chester, England) which put the fear of god in them, so much so, they immediately tripped and fell headfirst into the amphitheatre knocking themselves out cold. Believing they were cursed when in fact it was just drunken words the gypsy could not even remember ever saying, the local man met with a series of unfortunate events and lived a miserable life. Hodgepodge had seen him many times wandering around covered in bruises and supporting broken bones. The gypsy even tried to put things right by telling him it wasn't true, but the man still met with these disastrous occurrences.

So, in Hodgepodge's wisdom, he decided to play on the owner's fear of his magical powers and do the same. It worked and Mr. Pemberton bowed his head in defeat which was incredible from a man of his position. Surely, he didn't believe in Goblins and Folklore Associations?

It seemed he did!

"Five guesses," repeated Hodgepodge. He departed a stink which gave a sickening reminder as he left.

Oh he was good at this. He left the Mayor in such a quandary. The man was glad he felt better of course, but at what price?

Hodgepodge waited a week before Mr. Pemberton would come and talk to him about the matter again.

"Right, let's finish this."

"Before you start, I need you to sign this contract," said Hodgepodge, pulling out a grubby piece of paper from an unmentionable place about his person. He had scribbled an agreement which stated Mr. Pemberton had to sign over the whole rope business to him if he did not guess correctly where Hodgepodge lived after five attempts.

"Give it here," Mr. Pemberton snatched it and immediately signed it to the goblin's astonishment. He could see it now, sleek suits, servants – he could live like someone intelligent for a change and not a daft hoarder. Holidays, he suddenly thought. He could visit cousin Trumpypump in Australia and attach corks to his hat.

"So, would you like to start now?" he asked the man.

"Yes. Let's get this over with, it's simple. You don't have a home. You're a beggar," he looked smug. The answer was staring him in the face all this time. The little man looked destitute, he smelt like a tramp, he clearly was a homeless person.

"Wrong," smirked Hodgepodge.

"Right well - do you live in the city's Rows?"

These continuous half-timbered galleries which could be reached by steps and formed a second row of shops above those at street level, had lots of unmentionable things happen there in the darkened hours.

"It smells like you, so I imagined you must spend a lot of time there."

"Where would I sleep? It's so wooden and hard," said Hodgepodge.

"The Castle then?" Said the Mayor confidently. "They have dungeons which would accommodate your needs."

"No, certainly not!" Hodgepodge's face grew red. "I would have to share it with villains!" He was horrified at the thought.

The Mayor deliberated at his desk for a few minutes.

"Well I know it's not Billy Hobby's Well because you wouldn't smell like you do. You would be clean wouldn't you with all that water and you can't live in the Minerva Shrine's cave. There wouldn't be enough room for the two of you." He sat up straight, "I hope you are not counting these?"

The Goblin's lips were beginning to form an unnaturally wide curve.

"Of course not sir." He couldn't hide it any longer and did a little dance in his merriment. The man hadn't got a clue. He will have that desk and his fancy cups and saucers thrown out first when he takes over.

"I've got it!" he jumped up. "You live in the amphitheatre. It was built for animals and well… you would fit in perfectly around there. You might even become some sort of bizarre attraction of sorts."

Hodgepodge was not bothered by this comment. He clasped his hands together in happiness. Not only will he get his tower back but he will be the owner of the rope business.

"You only have one more guess," he bounced up and down to celebrate, so sure he was going to get the final answer wrong.

"You silly rascal!" retorted the man. His voice sounded much louder and sterner. "You live here, right under the floorboards!"

"Ahhhhh….How did you know?" Hodgepodge screeched. His whole new world came tumbling down around him like his hoard of rubbish.

"It wasn't difficult was it," he sat back down, placing his feet up on the table. "When we arrived here, we had to decontaminate the place. When you turned up smelling of the same smell, well, it didn't take much to work it out you were, to put it politely, residing somewhere within this building. I just had to find out where, and there weren't many places to look were there?"

The spright's face screwed up into something uglier. The disappointment made his stomach feel bad which wasn't good for the fresh air.

"You understand, I can't have you living in this building? The smell, it's - yes well, anyway, my customers may need to visit you see. That is why this morning, I had it all filled in."

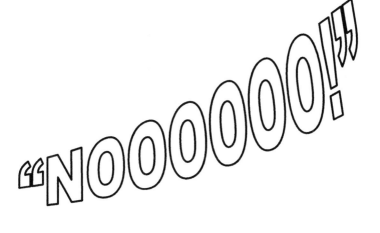

Hodgepodge screamed.

"What do you mean all filled in?"

"Good old concrete. We did not bother with removing the junk. No-one was willing to sort through it, but I guessed you wouldn't be bothered as it was just a load of rubbish so they poured concrete in there."

The coins! Hodgepodge was now in serious trouble. "They were my things!" He whimpered.

The Mayor had no idea what he had just done. It was an outrage.

"The good news is, it's improved the smell in here – well it had before you walked back in."

How would Hodgepodge explain this to the FA? He was in violation of his contract – he will be relegated for breach of trust and condemned to live in the city sewers for the rest of his life. It STUNK down there!

"But my offer still stands," John still needed the hard-working urchin. He was too valuable to him with his magic hands. He was convinced his offer was going to appeal to him.

"You can have that job for life and live here in the store shed outside with your very own beautifully hand-crafted chamber pot and a clean jug of water every single night."

"That was my home!" cried the Goblin. It wasn't the reaction John Pemberton was expecting.

"I will provide plenty of food," he added, thinking this would swing it for him.

The little creature lowered his head.

"…you can have all the clothes you need," it would be a life of luxury for someone like him. "A bathtub!" What a brilliant idea! He had surely won him over now, "I will get my men to boil water for you every evening so you can soak in a hot bath. It will improve the smell around this place and make it easier for us all to work with you. We will all be happy."

But the truth was, Hodgepodge was worthless to him now. All Hodgepodge could think about was his coins encased in a huge rock under the floorboards, his beautiful Goblin Tower with stunning views, highjacked and taken away from him, and the FA!

"HODGEPODGE!" The Mayor snapped. "Do you agree?"

Hodgepodge could not face the FA. There was no way he could stay here no matter what the Mayor offered him. With that, he turned and ran as fast as his smelly feet could take him.

The last time he was seen was on the Rows, then in the Castle's dungeon, and once hanging around Billy Hobby's Well only to be moved on. He did not bother with the Minerva Shrine as there wasn't enough room, and there wasn't enough shelter in the Amphitheatre. Then he disappeared.

People say the FA did eventually catch up with

him and he was doomed to a disgusting life in the city's sewers collecting things. Then in 1914, the priceless hoard of one hundred and twenty-two Anglo-Saxon silver coins were finally found in Pemberton's Parlour. Nobody knows who really put them there and rumour has it, that on a hot day, you can sometimes smell and hear a goblin in the city's sewers below.

The end.

We hope you enjoyed your tour of Chester!

Come back soon!

Find your way through the city to the Eastgate Clock. Watch out! It's a bit whiffy round here!

Clock Words Solution

```
F  A  C  E  .  .  .  .  T  I  C  K  T  O  C  K  .  .
P  T  C  .  .  .  .  .  .  .  .  .  .  .  .  .  .  .
E  .  I  L  C  L  O  C  K  M  A  K  E  R  .  .  .  H
N  B  .  M  O  .  .  .  .  .  .  .  .  .  .  .  .  O
D  T  I  .  E  C  .  .  .  .  .  .  .  .  .  .  .  U
U  .  I  G  .  K  K  T  I  M  E  P  I  E  C  E  .  R
L  .  .  C  B  .  E  S  .  .  .  .  .  .  .  .  .  G
U  .  .  .  K  E  .  E  M  H  A  N  D  S  .  .  .  L
M  .  .  .  .  I  N  .  P  I  .  .  .  .  .  .  .  A
.  .  .  .  .  .  N  .  .  E  T  .  .  .  .  .  .  S
.  .  .  .  .  .  .  G  .  .  R  H  .  .  .  .  .  S
.  E  A  S  T  G  A  T  E  C  L  O  C  K  .  .  .  .
```

BIG BEN (SE,2,4)
CLOCKMAKER (E,5,3)
CLOCKSMITH (SE,3,2)
EASTGATE CLOCK (E,2,12)
FACE (E,1,1)

HANDS (E,10,8)
HOURGLASS (S,18,3)
PENDULUM (S,1,2)
TICKING (SE,2,5)
TICK-TOCK (E,9,1)

TIMEKEEPER (SE,2,2)
TIMEPIECE (E,8,6)

Giant Words Solution

```
.  .  .  .  . H U M O N G O U S . M .
G I G A N T I C . . . . . . . I .
.  .  . M . . O G R E . . . . T G .
. V . O . . . . . . . . . I H .
.  . A N . I M M E N S E . . . T T .
.  .  . S . . . . . J U M B O . A Y .
.  .  . T T T R E M E N D O U S N . .
.  .  . R . . . . . . . . . . I . .
.  .  . O . . . . . . . . . C . .
.  .  . U . H U G E . . . . . . .
.  .  . S . . . . . . . . . . .
. M A S S I V E . . . . . . . .
```

GIGANTIC (E,1,2)
HUGE (E,6,10)
HUMONGOUS (E,7,1)
IMMENSE (E,6,5)
JUMBO (E,10,6)

MASSIVE (E,2,12)
MIGHTY (S,17,1)
MONSTROUS (S,4,3)
OGRE (E,7,3)
TITANIC (S,16,3)

TREMENDOUS (E,6,7)
VAST (SE,2,4)

Smelly Words Solution

```
E   .   .   .   W   H   I   F   F   Y   .   P   .   .   .   R   .
V   R   .   .   .   .   .   .   .   .   .   .   O   .   .   O   .
I   .   E   .   .   .   .   .   .   .   .   .   N   .   T   .
L   .   .   E   S   M   E   L   L   Y   .   .   S   .   .   G   T   .
S   .   P   .   K   .   .   F   .   .   .   T   .   R   .   E   .
M   .   U   .   .   I   .   .   O   .   .   .   I   .   .   A   N   .
E   .   T   .   .   N   .   .   U   .   .   N   .   .   .   N   .
L   .   R   .   .   .   G   .   .   L   .   K   .   .   .   .   K
L   .   I   S   T   R   O   N   G   S   M   E   L   L   I   N   G   .
I   .   D   .   .   .   .   .   .   .   .   .   .   .   .   .
N   .   .   .   R   A   N   C   I   D   .   .   .   .   .   .
G   .   .   .   .   .   .   .   .   .   .   .   .   .   .   .
```

EVIL-SMELLING (S,1,1)
FOUL (SE,8,5)
PONG (SE,13,1)
PUTRID (S,3,5)
RANCID (E,5,11)

RANK (SE,15,5)
REEKING (SE,2,2)
ROTTEN (S,17,1)
SMELLY (E,5,4)
STINK (S,13,4)

STRONG-SMELLING (E,4,9)
WHIFFY (E,6,1)

Tiny Words Solution

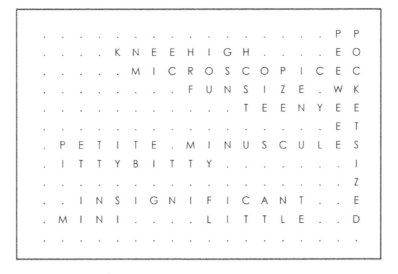

```
.  .  .  .  .  .  .  .  .  .  .  .  .  .  .  P  P
.  .  .  .  K  N  E  E  H  I  G  H  .  .  .  .  E  O
.  .  .  .  .  M  I  C  R  O  S  C  O  P  I  C  E  C
.  .  .  .  .  .  .  F  U  N  S  I  Z  E  .  W  K
.  .  .  .  .  .  .  .  .  .  T  E  E  N  Y  E  E
.  .  .  .  .  .  .  .  .  .  .  .  .  .  .  E  T
.  P  E  T  I  T  E  .  M  I  N  U  S  C  U  L  E  S
.  I  T  T  Y  B  I  T  T  Y  .  .  .  .  .  .  .  I
.  .  .  .  .  .  .  .  .  .  .  .  .  .  .  .  .  Z
.  .  I  N  S  I  G  N  I  F  I  C  A  N  T  .  .  E
.  M  I  N  I  .  .  .  .  .  L  I  T  T  L  E  .  .  D
.  .  .  .  .  .  .  .  .  .  .  .  .  .  .  .  .  .
```

FUN-SIZE (E,9,4)
INSIGNIFICANT (E,3,10)
ITTY-BITTY (E,2,8)
KNEE-HIGH (E,5,2)
LITTLE (E,10,11)

MICROSCOPIC (E,6,3)
MINI (E,2,11)
MINUSCULE (E,9,7)
PEEWEE (S,17,1)
PETITE (E,2,7)

POCKET-SIZED (S,18,1)
TEENY (E,12,5)

159

www.evelynwinters.co.uk

Visit the Teachers and Parents page by scanning here:

Printed in Great Britain
by Amazon